In Memory of

Melissa M. Gray

by

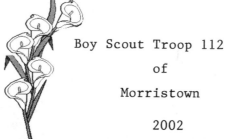

Boy Scout Troop 112

of

Morristown

2002

FIELD TRIPS

BUG HUNTING • ANIMAL TRACKING

with

JIM ARNOSKY

BIRD–WATCHING • SHORE WALKING •

HarperCollinsPublishers

Field Trips
Copyright © 2002 by Jim Arnosky
Printed in the U.S.A. All rights reserved.
www.harperchildrens.com

Library of Congress Cataloging-in-Publication Data
Arnosky, Jim.
Field trips : bug hunting, animal tracking, bird-watching,
and shore walking with Jim Arnosky.
p.   cm.
ISBN 0-688-15172-8 — ISBN 0-688-15173-6 (lib. bdg.)
1. Natural history—Field work—Juvenile literature.
2. Nature study—Activity programs—Juvenile literature.
[1. Natural history.   2. Nature study.]   I. Title.
QH51 .A74 2002   508—dc21
00-069721   CIP
AC

Typography by Stephanie Bart-Horvath
2 3 4 5 6 7 8 9 10
❖
First Edition

This book is dedicated
to Roger Tory Peterson,
whose wonderful field guides
have accompanied nature lovers
on field trips all around
the world.

CONTENTS

Introduction 6

CHAPTER 1
Bug Hunting 9

- Identifying Bugs 13
- Bug-Hunting Equipment 14
- Ticks 16
- Recording Findings 20
- Cases, Cocoons, and Chrysalises 22
- Bug Hunting at Night 24

CHAPTER 2
Animal Tracking 31

- Track Sets 34
- Perfect Footprints 36
- Tracking Safety 40
- Recording Tracks 42
- Reptile Tracks 47

CONTENTS

CHAPTER 3

Bird-watching 53

- Identifying Birds 56
- Field Marks 58
- Bird Behavior 60
- Keeping a Notebook 62
- Rare Bird Sightings 66

CHAPTER 4

Shore Walking 73

- Types of Shoreland 76
- Plant Succession 78
- Shore-Walking Safety 82
- A Shore Walker's Notebook 84
- Found Objects 86
- Fossil Finds 88
- Underwater Plants 89
- Shoreline Trees 90

Index 95

INTRODUCTION

As far back as I can remember, I have been fascinated by wildlife. The very first drawing I recall making was a picture of a turtle with a colorful shell. Even as a little boy, I wondered about life in the wild. I wanted to know all the birds and bugs and learn to identify animal tracks. But I was alone in my wonder. No one else in my family shared my interest in wild things. Luckily, we lived near fields and woods, and I could spend whole days outdoors, exploring.

You can learn a lot about nature on your own. But it is more fun to learn with someone else. A walk with a friend, a hike with your family, a day afield with classmates can all be shared learning experiences, and the sharing makes them special.

For parents and teachers planning a trip outdoors with your children, and for all you young naturalists discovering and learning on your own, I have written this book. Each chapter focuses on a separate field-trip goal—bug hunting, animal tracking, bird-watching, and shore walking. You can plan a field trip around one chapter's activity or use information in all four chapters for a field trip of general nature appreciation. Besides a good pair of binoculars, every field tripper should carry a notebook and pencil. There are examples to show you how to start your own field-trip notebook. And each chapter includes charts for the quick identification of many species.

Now, pull on your hiking boots, grab your binoculars, and get your notebook and pencil. We're going on a field trip!

Jim Arnosky

Ramtails 2002

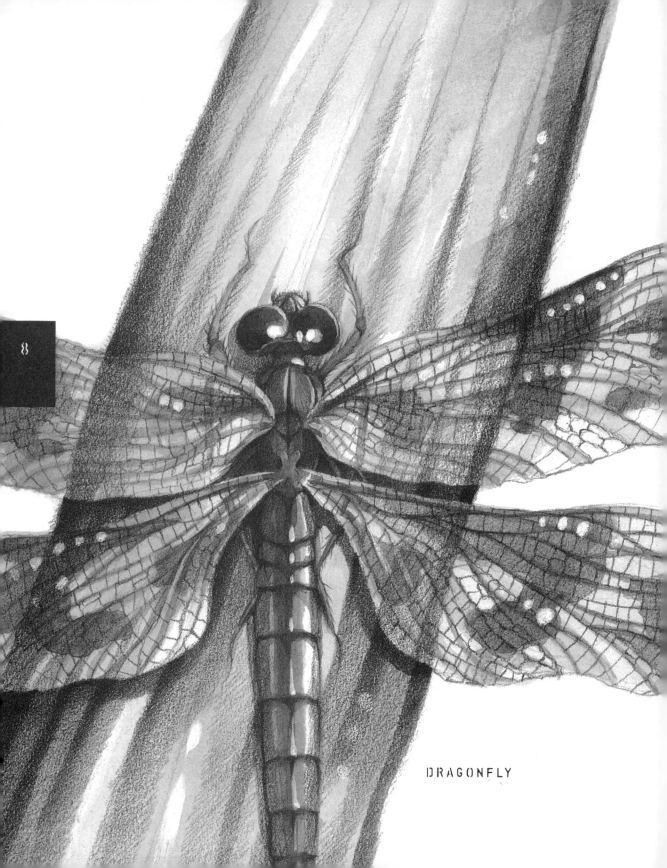

DRAGONFLY

1

BUG HUNTING

I remember my first real field trip. I was seven years old. A friend and his father were going on a nature hike, and I was invited! We walked to the end of the road, passed the last house in our village, and followed a narrow path through a wild, brush-covered field. On the leaves of the bushes were hundreds of great big strange-looking insects. They were cicadas. I followed my friend as he followed his father through the tangle of stems and branches until we were surrounded by the giant bugs. We watched them fly from plant to plant, sometimes buzzing right past our ears. We collected a few and put them in a jar. I felt as if I was in some faraway jungle. It was my first truly wild experience.

Today I have a grandson who is seven years old. Together we walk the long winding footpaths around the farm, looking for caterpillars, butterflies, dragonflies, grasshoppers, beetles, and spiders, and for a time my grandson and I are lost in wonder.

If you cannot let a butterfly flutter by without following it a little ways . . . If you have ever spent time watching a spider weave its web . . . If you have trapped a firefly in a jar just to look closely at its mysterious glowing abdomen, before letting it fly again . . . If you find ants, beetles, caterpillars, and dragonflies mesmerizing . . . you are a born bug hunter!

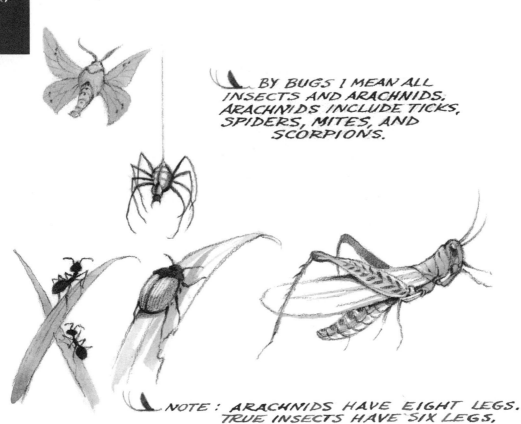

BY BUGS I MEAN ALL INSECTS AND ARACHNIDS. ARACHNIDS INCLUDE TICKS, SPIDERS, MITES, AND SCORPIONS.

NOTE: ARACHNIDS HAVE EIGHT LEGS. TRUE INSECTS HAVE SIX LEGS.

Anywhere you look outdoors, you are likely to see some bug flying or crawling around. On a bug-hunting field trip, you can choose to look for insects or spiders in a general way. Or you can go out to find and watch a certain species, such as a favorite butterfly.

MONARCH
BUTTERFLY
AND
MONARCH
CATERPILLAR

There are bugs to look for indoors, also. Spiders are making webs in skyscraper windows. Houseplants are home to tiny flies, mites, spiders, earwigs, aphids, and ants. Occasionally a ladybug may be discovered climbing a green leaf of a potted plant or scaling window glass. I once found a daddy longlegs in our bathtub!

You can catalog the tiny creatures living in your house or classroom. Then go on a field trip and see if you can find the same species living outdoors.

LADYBUG ON
HOUSEPLANT

IDENTIFYING BUGS

Just how many different kinds of bugs are in the world is unknown. We do know that there are more insects on earth than all other kinds of animals combined. However, even with so many different species, the basic types of bugs are easy to recognize. Generally, bugs can be divided into three main groups—land-dwelling bugs (which, besides a multitude of insects, includes all arachnids), airborne (flying) bugs, and aquatic (water-dwelling) bugs. Knowing this not only helps you identify bugs more easily but also helps you locate the bugs you are looking for.

LAND

AIRBORNE

AQUATIC

BUG-HUNTING EQUIPMENT

Unlike birds and other wildlife, bugs are not shy. They will crawl or fly all around you. I've done some of my best bug watching while trout fishing, observing close-up mayflies and caddis flies that have alighted on my sleeve or hand.

For viewing tiny bugs afield, I carry a pocket magnifying lens. A small aquarium net comes in handy for gently scooping up aquatic insects for a closer look.

You can use a small plastic jar to carry home pieces of wings or shed insect skins or even a dead insect you find. A pair of tweezers will help you to pick up such small and often delicate things.

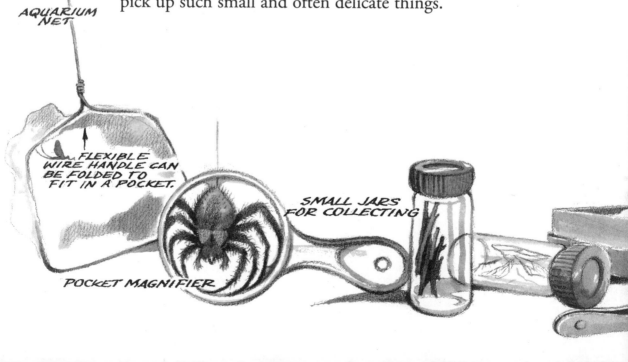

AQUARIUM NET

FLEXIBLE WIRE HANDLE CAN BE FOLDED TO FIT IN A POCKET.

POCKET MAGNIFIER

SMALL JARS FOR COLLECTING

These found objects are fascinating to examine closely later at home. With a magnifying lens or a microscope, even the tiniest fly looks monstrous!

Using binoculars for watching bugs!

On a field trip, a 7 x 35 power binoculars can bring you closer to large insects without you having to chase after them. I often use my binoculars to watch bugs, the same way I watch birds. And using binoculars is the only safe way to get a close look at stinging scorpions or hornets and biting ants.

Always stay at least twelve feet from an ant mound unless you are certain the ants are not a biting kind. Stay well away from any tree or bush or hole you suspect to be home to a beehive or hornet nest.

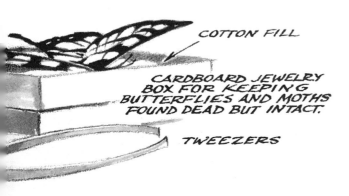

COTTON FILL

CARDBOARD JEWELRY BOX FOR KEEPING BUTTERFLIES AND MOTHS FOUND DEAD BUT INTACT.

TWEEZERS

TICKS

When I'm bug hunting, I'm always careful about ticks. I stay to the edges of the tall plants and grasses and walk only on the short, mowed grass of a lawn or the well-worn paths in the woods. If you do not rub against a plant a tick happens to be on, chances are the tick will not be able to climb on you.

Apply insect repellant to exposed skin and around the cuffs of your pants and sleeves.

Wear a hat so ticks that may be on leaves above you will not be able to drop down onto your hair.

WHEN WALKING IN TALL GRASS OR WEEDS, TUCK YOUR PANTS INTO YOUR SOCKS AS A PRECAUTION AGAINST TICKS.

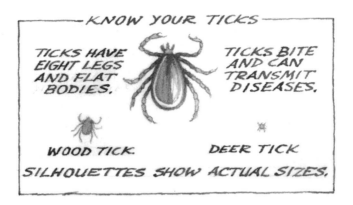

KNOW YOUR TICKS

TICKS HAVE EIGHT LEGS AND FLAT BODIES.

TICKS BITE AND CAN TRANSMIT DISEASES.

WOOD TICK

DEER TICK

SILHOUETTES SHOW ACTUAL SIZES.

Be aware of the possible presence of tiny ticks in your yard or garden. If you happen to brush through tall grass or weeds, take a moment to stop and check your clothes for ticks. If you find any, get them off using the tweezers in your bug-hunting gear—or flick them off with a twig—before they can crawl and migrate to your skin.

Remember, the tick must come off intact. Never squeeze, crush, or break a tick when removing one. Some ticks carry diseases that can be transmitted to humans.

A bee, wasp, or hornet flying in a straight line is usually leaving its home or returning to it. Whenever I see one of these stinging insects flying in a straight line, I quickly determine the direction it came from and the direction it is headed and then avoid both.

THOUGH THEY LOOK FEARSOME, DRAGONFLIES AND THEIR KIN DO NOT STING OR BITE PEOPLE.

The best place to hunt bugs is in a garden. Any planting of flowers or vegetables attracts scores of flies, beetles, ants, spiders, caterpillars, and butterflies. By midsummer, when the plants are high, grasshopper populations explode. Every step you take can send one or two grasshoppers jumping.

BALD-FACED HORNET

PAPER WASP

YELLOW JACKET

HONEY BEE

LEARN WHICH BUGS IN YOUR AREA DO STING OR BITE AND AVOID THEM. ABOVE ARE FOUR OF THE MOST COMMON.

RECORDING FINDINGS

Most of the smaller bugs you find can be sketched life-sized and written about on one page of your field notes. Larger insects may take two pages. First record the identity of the bug. If you know the proper name—i.e., *Dragonfly*—write it down. If you are not certain of the bug's exact identity, write down whether you think it is a fly, beetle, caterpillar, etc. Next, record the location and whether the bug is on the ground, a stone, a grass blade, or flower; hovering in the air; or floating on or swimming in the water.

Draw even the largest bugs full size, even if you have to stretch your drawing across the gutter of your notebook onto the next page. Take time to add every detail you see, such as segmented abdomens, jointed legs, wing veins, antennae, body bristles, and hairs.

SEPTEMBER 1

CRINKLE COVE
LAKE CHAMPLAIN

DRAGONFLY

THIS DRAGONFLY HAD A
LARGE HEAD ON A
NARROW NECK.

EACH WING IS
DELICATELY VEINED
LIKE THIS.

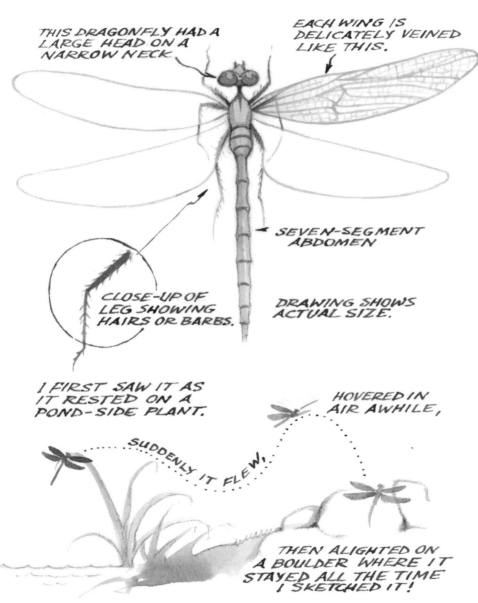

SEVEN-SEGMENT
ABDOMEN

CLOSE-UP OF
LEG SHOWING
HAIRS OR BARBS.

DRAWING SHOWS
ACTUAL SIZE.

I FIRST SAW IT AS
IT RESTED ON A
POND-SIDE PLANT.

HOVERED IN
AIR AWHILE,

SUDDENLY IT FLEW,

THEN ALIGHTED ON
A BOULDER WHERE IT
STAYED ALL THE TIME
I SKETCHED IT!

CASES, COCOONS, AND CHRYSALISES

The objects bugs make, such as webs, cocoons, and even mobile homes, are interesting. To protect themselves in their rugged stream environment, the larvae of caddis flies make cases to hide in, using various natural materials. The caddis cases, as they are called, are truly mobile homes, because caddis larvae drag their cases from place to place. For bug hunters, the best thing about caddis cases is that they are usually found in water less than one foot deep and often are close to the stream bank. You can stay safely on the bank and pick a case out of the stream to look more closely.

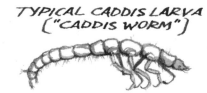

TYPICAL CADDIS LARVA ("CADDIS WORM")

CADDIS FLY

SILHOUETTE SHOWS ACTUAL SIZE.

A NEAT RECTANGULAR CASE MADE OF THIN STRIPS OF LEAVES

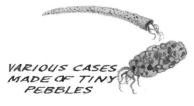

VARIOUS CASES MADE OF TINY PEBBLES

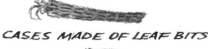

CASES MADE OF LEAF BITS

STICK CASE

If the case is empty, the caddis larva has abandoned it to emerge as a winged caddis fly. You can bring the empty caddis case home. If the case still has the caddis larva in it, put the case back in the stream.

Moth caterpillars construct or spin variously shaped cocoons in which to hibernate and change into winged moths. The changing process is called metamorphosis. A butterfly caterpillar undergoes metamorphosis in a hard-shelled case called a chrysalis. It's okay to bring a cocoon or chrysalis home from a field trip and watch as the moth or butterfly emerges, as long as you release it afterward.

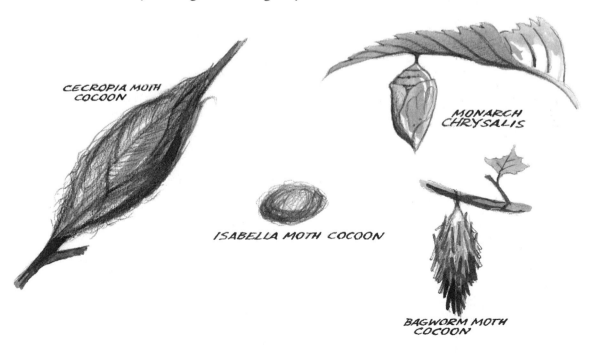

CECROPIA MOTH COCOON

MONARCH CHRYSALIS

ISABELLA MOTH COCOON

BAGWORM MOTH COCOON

BUG HUNTING AT NIGHT

At night, without ever leaving your doorstep or porch, you can attract many moths and other flying bugs simply by turning on a bright flashlight and keeping it still. After spending a whole day hunting for bugs, it's nice to have the bugs come and find you!

TRY HOLDING A FLASH~
LIGHT SHINING UPWARD
JUST BELOW A SPIDER'S
WEB. YOU'LL SEE HOW
SPARKLING THE SILKEN
STRANDS OF A SPIDER
WEB CAN BE.

Using my silhouette charts on this and the following pages, you will be able to identify almost every type of bug you see and make your next field trip your "buggiest" ever!

MOTH

MOTH AT REST

BUTTERFLY

BUTTERFLY
AT REST

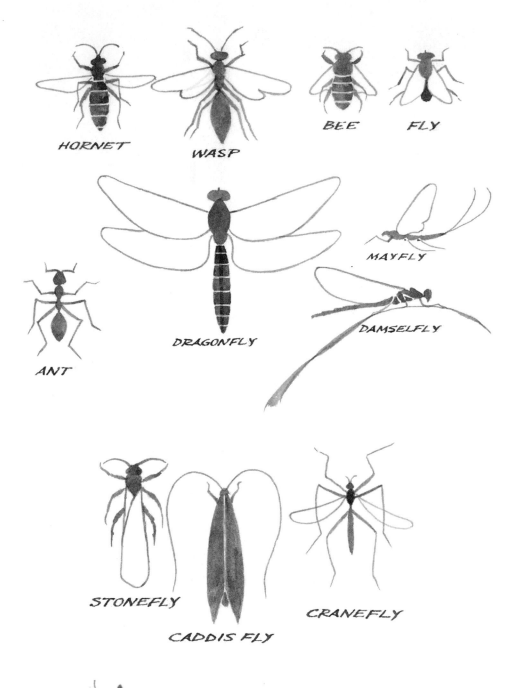

HORNET

WASP

BEE

FLY

ANT

DRAGONFLY

MAYFLY

DAMSELFLY

STONEFLY

CADDIS FLY

CRANEFLY

NOTE: ACTUAL SIZES WILL VARY
GREATLY FROM SPECIES TO
SPECIES.

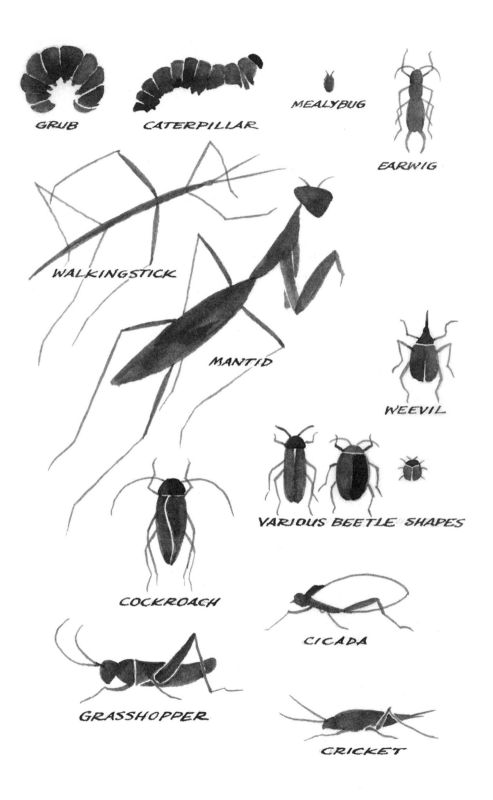

GRUB

CATERPILLAR

MEALYBUG

EARWIG

WALKINGSTICK

MANTID

WEEVIL

VARIOUS BEETLE SHAPES

COCKROACH

CICADA

GRASSHOPPER

CRICKET

TERMITE

MOSQUITO

GNAT

UNDERWATER BUGS

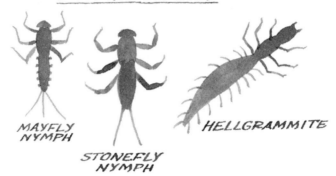

MAYFLY
NYMPH

STONEFLY
NYMPH

HELLGRAMMITE

DRAGONFLY
NAIAD

CADDIS WORM
[LARVA]
IN STICK CASE

WATER SURFACE BUGS

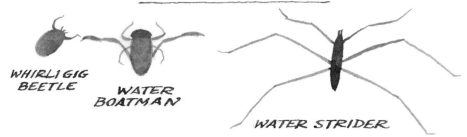

WHIRLIGIG
BEETLE

WATER
BOATMAN

WATER STRIDER

ARACHNIDS

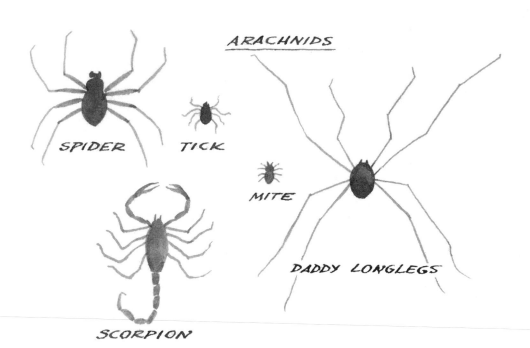

SPIDER

TICK

MITE

DADDY LONGLEGS

SCORPION

MOUNTAIN LION

2

ANIMAL TRACKING

Long before I began to find, photograph, and sketch wild animals, I studied their tracks. Many of the first wildlife scenes I drew or painted were created solely from the animal tracks I had found and followed. One of those early paintings was purchased by a nationally known wildlife photographer named Leonard Lee Rue. We have been friends ever since.

Leonard Lee Rue was the first to personally share his knowledge of wildlife with me. He is an expert on animal tracks, and I have asked him many questions. In answering, he explained much about the lives and behavior of the animals. We have had long discussions about moose tracks, deer tracks, bear tracks, and even lion tracks. Having him as a friend and teacher helped make the track studies in my journals more detailed, accurate, and informative.

My track teacher passed his knowledge on to me. In turn, I'd like to share my knowledge of animal tracks with you.

The footprints and other marks mammals, birds, reptiles, and insects make as they walk or crawl overland are called animal tracks. Because each species of animal has its own unique foot shape, it is possible to identify almost any animal from just one of its footprints.

If you are always noticing footprints in your yard, on woodland paths, and on dusty trails, you are an animal tracker.

DEER

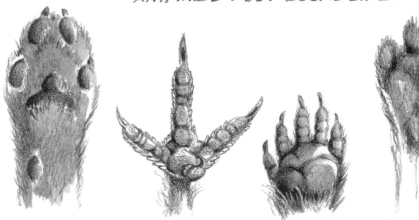

AN ANIMAL'S FOOTPRINT SHOWS WHAT THE BOTTOM OF THE ANIMAL'S FOOT LOOKS LIKE.

FOX   GROUSE   RACCOON   RABBIT

In warm seasons, look for animal tracks on wet beaches, shorelines, and moist woodland paths. In these places, the ground is soft enough to be imprinted by the pressing of footsteps, yet still firm enough to safely walk on. In dry areas, look for animal tracks in loose sand or in dust that coats the hard-packed soil of trails. If you live in snow country, you don't have to go far or anyplace special to find animal tracks in winter. In snow country animal tracks are everywhere.

ONE ANIMAL CAN CREATE A VARIETY OF MARKS, ESPECIALLY IN SOFT SAND OR SNOW.

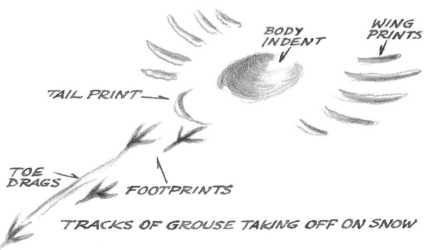

BODY INDENT

WING PRINTS

TAIL PRINT

TOE DRAGS

FOOTPRINTS

TRACKS OF GROUSE TAKING OFF ON SNOW

TRACK SETS

Wherever you find a single animal track, search on the ground around it for other tracks to make the set. In birds, a set of tracks consists of a right and left footprint. In four-footed animals, a set of tracks includes left and right front and left and right hind footprints.

HOUSE CAT FOOTPRINT AND FOUR-TRACK SET

BLUE JAY FOOTPRINT AND TWO-TRACK SET

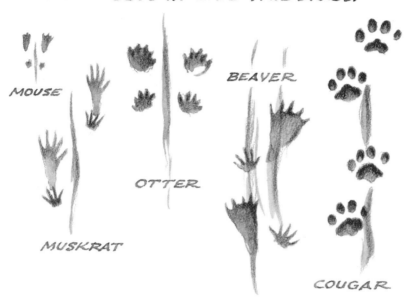

IN SNOW, SAND, OR MUD, SOME ANIMALS' TRACK SETS INCLUDE TAIL DRAGS.

MOUSE

MUSKRAT

OTTER

BEAVER

COUGAR

After you find one set of animal tracks, it is easy to locate another, and another, in the line of traveling tracks. Don't be tempted to follow unless you are with a guide or field-trip leader who knows the area well. An animal's tracks may lead to unfamiliar surroundings and can get you lost. One set of tracks will tell you all you need to know.

PERFECT FOOTPRINTS

A single clearly pressed footprint can reveal the identity of the track maker. And a complete set of tracks
will show whether the animal was walking, running,
hopping, sliding, or simply standing still.

WHEN FOUR-
LEGGED ANIMALS
HOP, JUMP, OR
BOUND, THEIR
HIND PRINTS
REGISTER IN
FRONT OF THE
FRONT PRINTS
ON EACH LANDING.

RABBIT TRACKS

WHEN I FIND TRACKS OF AN
ANIMAL HOPPING, I LIKE
TO MEASURE THE DISTANCE
THE ANIMAL HOPPED.

STANDING TRACKS
ARE ALWAYS
FOLLOWED BY
MOTION TRACKS.

TRACKS OF A FOUR-LEGGED ANIMAL STANDING
STILL FORM A RECTANGLE OR A SQUARE.

IN WALKING TRACKS, THE FOOTPRINTS
ARE EVENLY SPACED IN TRACK SET AFTER SET.

TRACKS OF
AN ANIMAL
RUNNING ARE
CLOSELY SPACED
AND OFTEN SHOW
OVERPRINTING
OF FOOTPRINTS.

RUNNING TRACK
SETS ARE SPACED
A SMALL LEAP APART.

Some animals' footprints are so uniquely shaped or fall in such a pattern that they can be identified at a glance. Deer hoofprints are heart shaped. Raccoon prints resemble tiny human hands and feet. Sets of fox tracks join to create long straight dotted lines, and sets of skunk tracks each make a neat diagonal pattern. All of these tracks are easily recognizable, especially in snow.

RACCOON
TRACKS

STRIPED
SKUNK
TRACKS

DEER
TRACKS

LINE OF FOX TRACKS IN SNOW

Other animals' tracks need to be studied more closely before they can be identified. Feline (the cat family) and canine (the dog family) footprints may look similar. But upon close inspection, you will see that, because of their retractable claws, feline footprints usually lack nail marks.

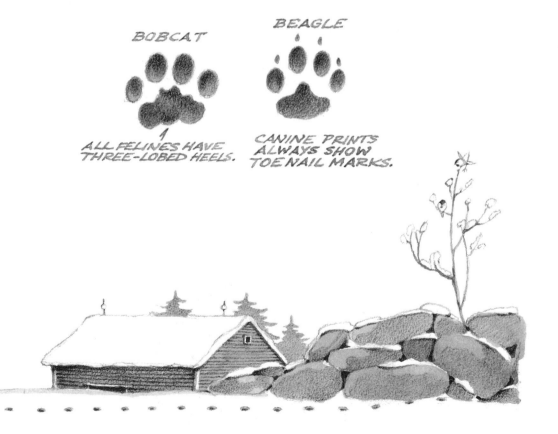

BOBCAT

BEAGLE

ALL FELINES HAVE THREE-LOBED HEELS.

CANINE PRINTS ALWAYS SHOW TOE NAIL MARKS.

TRACKING SAFETY

Usually, by the time you discover an animal's tracks, the animal will have been long gone. If, however, by some rare coincidence, you do see an animal at the end of its tracks, back away and leave the animal alone. If cornered, even a small, harmless animal will defend itself.

ALLIGATOR TRACKS ON MUD

If you happen to live in an area of the country where large, powerful animals such as bears, moose, cougars, or alligators are known to live, learn to recognize these animals' tracks. Then, if you ever happen to see such tracks, you will know immediately to retreat and stay away. You will find examples of cougar, bear, and moose tracks at the end of this chapter. Alligator tracks are shown below.

RECORDING TRACKS

In your field-trip notebook, record the animal tracks you find by making a small sketch of one entire footprint. Then mark it with its measurements—length and width. The proper way to measure the length of an animal's footprint is from the top of the longest toe (not including any toenail marks) to the back of the heel. Measure width from the outside of the widest part of the print to the outside of the opposite side. Be sure to draw any toenail marks. If the animal has hooves, sketch the shape accurately. To record a whole set of tracks, draw a tiny diagram of the set showing each footprint in its precise placement within the set. Beside your sketches of animal tracks, you might like to write down all the details about where and when you found the tracks.

SAMPLE TRACK PAGE

WHITE-TAILED DEER   JUNE 5

I WAS ON MY WAY TO THE POND WHEN I SAW THE HOOFPRINTS OF A DOE AND FAWN.

3" LONG

2.5" WIDE

HOOFPRINT IN SOFT SAND

38" WALKING SET

12" STEPS

FAWN TRACKS

1.75"

1.5"

FAWN'S PRINT

THE FAWN MUST HAVE BEEN ONLY DAYS OLD. ITS TRACKS WERE SO TINY!

How fresh is the track?

It takes skill and practice to be able to accurately guess the freshness of an animal's tracks. The easiest way is to visit the same familiar spots day after day. You will quickly notice any new footprints that have been made since your last visit. Watching the way tracks in snow change and become distorted as the snow melts is another easy way to determine the freshness of tracks.

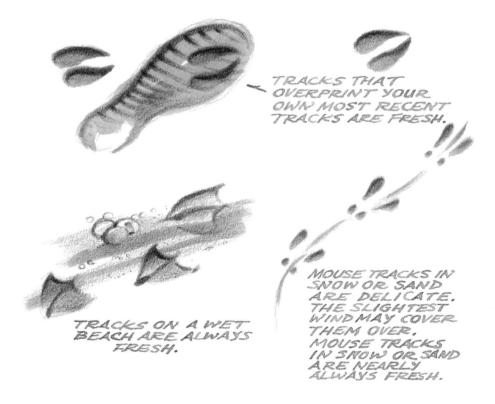

TRACKS THAT OVERPRINT YOUR OWN MOST RECENT TRACKS ARE FRESH.

TRACKS ON A WET BEACH ARE ALWAYS FRESH.

MOUSE TRACKS IN SNOW OR SAND ARE DELICATE. THE SLIGHTEST WIND MAY COVER THEM OVER. MOUSE TRACKS IN SNOW OR SAND ARE NEARLY ALWAYS FRESH.

🐾 *MELTING SNOW TRACKS*

AS SNOW MELTS, ANIMAL TRACKS PRINTED
IN THE SNOW ENLARGE AND BECOME
VERY DISTORTED.

DOG TRACKS BEGIN TO RESEMBLE TRACKS
OF WOLVES OR BEARS.

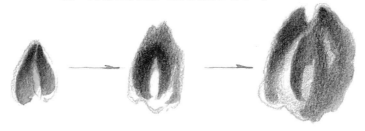

DEER TRACKS ENLARGE AND LOOK MORE
LIKE MOOSE TRACKS.

AND SETS OF RABBIT TRACKS MELT TOGETHER
AND SUGGEST GIANT FOOTPRINTS.

🐾 CONSIDER HOW MUCH A TRACK
HAS MELTED AND ENLARGED
BEFORE CONCLUDING THAT
"BIGFOOT" IS IN YOUR TOWN.

About dewclaws

Many mammals have dewclaws, which are small hind toes high up on the feet. In pawed animals, dewclaws are mostly functionless, and they rarely show in tracks. Hoofed animals actually use their dewclaws for added stability when walking on ice or in mud or deep snow, and when running at great speed. During these times, dewclaws register in tracks, directly behind the hoofprints.

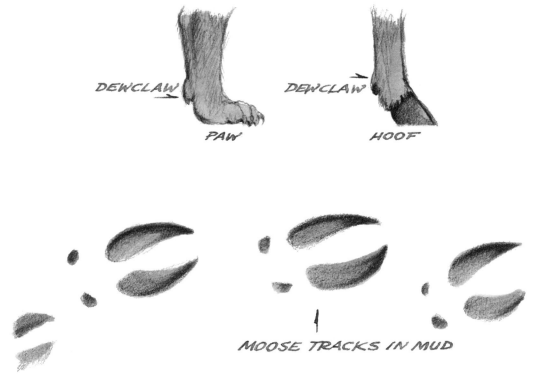

MOOSE TRACKS IN MUD

REPTILE TRACKS

Occasionally you will find marks or prints that don't match any mammal or bird tracks. More often than not, mysterious tracks are reptilian in origin. Here are three common reptile tracks to look for. Each shows hind foot (h.) and forefoot (f.) placement.

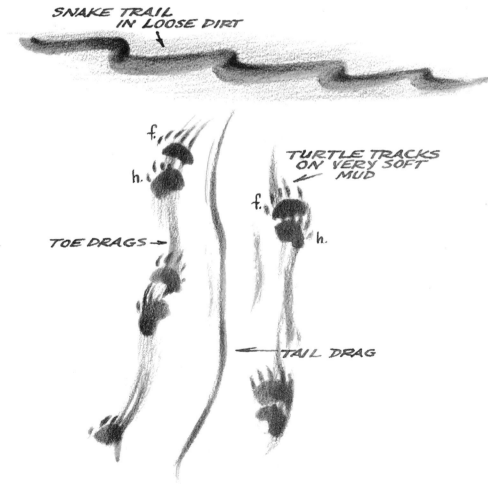

LIZARD TRACKS WITH TAIL DRAG

f.

h.

f.

h.

SNAKE TRAIL IN LOOSE DIRT

f.

h.

TURTLE TRACKS ON VERY SOFT MUD

f.

h.

TOE DRAGS

TAIL DRAG

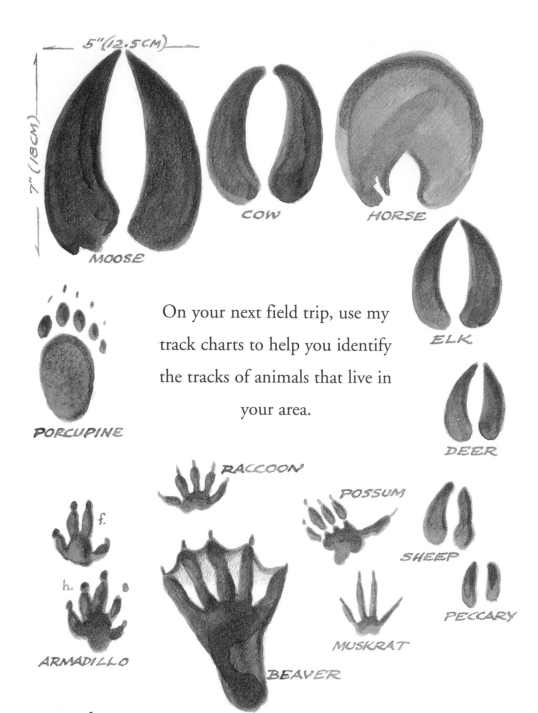

5"(12.5CM)

7"(18CM)

MOOSE

COW

HORSE

ELK

DEER

PORCUPINE

On your next field trip, use my track charts to help you identify the tracks of animals that live in your area.

RACCOON

POSSUM

f.

h.

ARMADILLO

BEAVER

MUSKRAT

SHEEP

PECCARY

NOTE: ALL TRACKS ARE SHOWN IN SIZE PROPORTION TO THE OTHER TRACKS ON THE SAME PAGE.

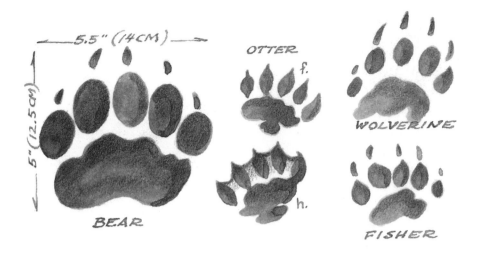

5.5" (14CM)

5" (12.5CM)

BEAR

OTTER

f.

h.

WOLVERINE

FISHER

WOLF

DOG (COLLIE SIZE)

COYOTE

RED FOX

GRAY FOX

49

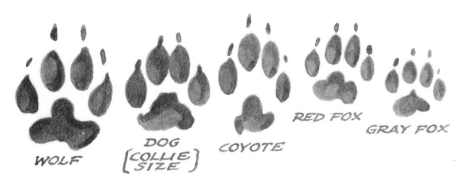

COUGAR

LYNX

BOBCAT

HOUSE CAT

NOTE: CAT TRACKS RARELY SHOW CLAW MARKS.

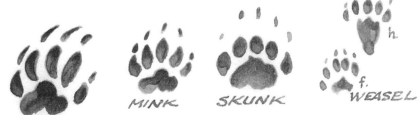

BADGER

MINK

SKUNK

WEASEL

h.

f.

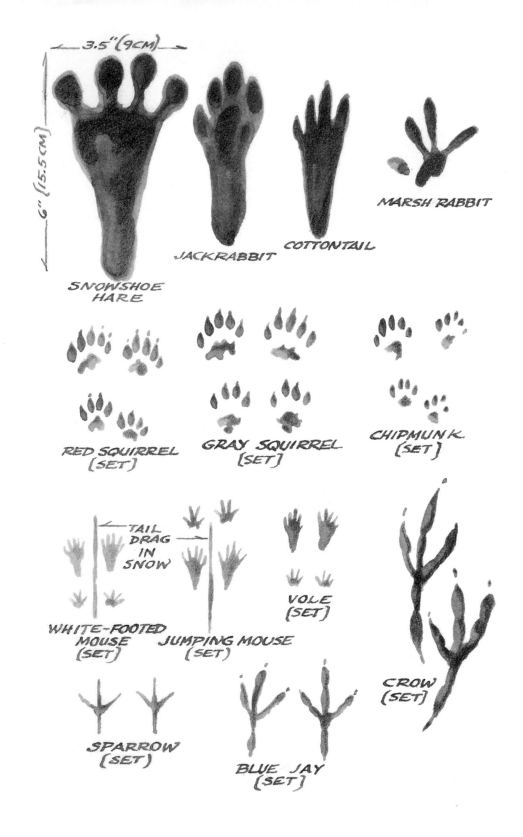

3.5" (9CM)

6" (15.5 CM)

SNOWSHOE
HARE

JACKRABBIT

COTTONTAIL

MARSH RABBIT

RED SQUIRREL
(SET)

GRAY SQUIRREL
(SET)

CHIPMUNK
(SET)

TAIL
DRAG
IN
SNOW

WHITE-FOOTED
MOUSE
(SET)

JUMPING MOUSE
(SET)

VOLE
(SET)

CROW
(SET)

SPARROW
(SET)

BLUE JAY
(SET)

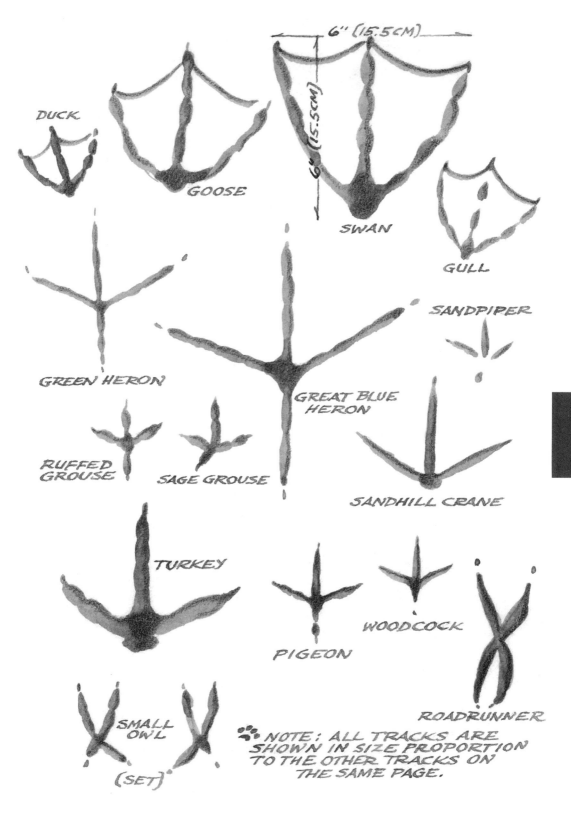

DUCK

GOOSE

6" (15.5CM)

6" (15.5CM)

SWAN

GULL

GREEN HERON

GREAT BLUE HERON

SANDPIPER

RUFFED GROUSE

SAGE GROUSE

SANDHILL CRANE

TURKEY

PIGEON

WOODCOCK

ROADRUNNER

SMALL OWL

(SET)

NOTE: ALL TRACKS ARE SHOWN IN SIZE PROPORTION TO THE OTHER TRACKS ON THE SAME PAGE.

51

52

PILEATED
WOODPECKER

3

BIRD-WATCHING

My first bird-watching teachers were authors. I read all the writings of John Burroughs. When I discovered his nature books, penned in the late nineteenth and early twentieth centuries, he was long gone. But John Burroughs's words of advice and his love of birds had lived on. I gobbled up descriptions of the wood thrush, screech owl, and kingfisher, wanting to see these birds for myself.

Roger Tory Peterson's bird guides helped me identify every bird I saw until I knew them all by heart. Peterson's paintings of birds accentuated each species' identifying marks, such as streaks of white on a pileated woodpecker's cheeks or dark bars on a mallard's wings. Having a Peterson field guide in your backpack was almost like having the author right there with you, pointing things out.

Remembering the wealth of information I gained from these early teachers, I have attempted to share observations and ideas that will help you enjoy bird-watching as much as I do.

Birds are everywhere! We see them on our way to school or work and find ourselves stopping to watch, even when we are busy doing other things. Birds are the easiest wild animals to find. They are conspicuous in flight, and they draw attention to themselves with their calls and songs.

Look for birds around water, where they come to drink, bathe, or feed on water plants and insects. Watch for birds near bushes, in fields or woods, along roadsides—any place where there is cover for them to hide or nest in.

Some species of birds can adapt to almost any environment. For instance, sparrows can live in many different kinds of places—from city streets to wilderness areas. Other species have specific habitat requirements. Woodpeckers thrive only where there are plenty of dead or dying trees to peck and dig into in search of wood-boring insects to eat. One thing's for certain: wherever you are, wherever you go, you will find birds.

PILEATED WOODPECKER

IDENTIFYING BIRDS

There are about as many kinds of birds as there are places birds are found. There are perching birds, climbing birds, gliding birds, and soaring birds. There are shorebirds and water birds. Many species of birds can be recognized by shape alone. Other species can be identified quickly by their colors. The brilliant red of a cardinal, for instance, is unmistakable.

Learn the parts of a bird and look for identifying colors or markings in the crown or crest, cheek, neck, breast, wing, rump, or tail. Knowing these parts of bird anatomy will help you identify the birds you see.

In some birds certain parts are exaggerated. For example, there are birds with exceptionally tall crests on their heads, such as cardinals, jays, and hooded mergansers, or tremendously long tails, such as scissortail flycatchers and roadrunners.

While I've pictured a wood duck for your reference, the parts are typical of almost every other type of bird.

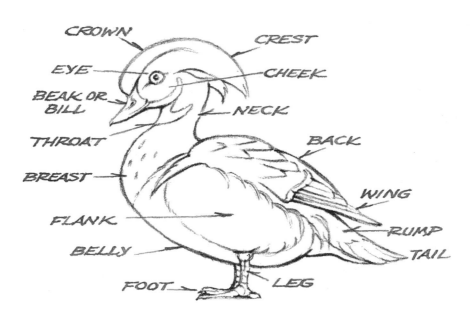

WHEN DESCRIBING BIRDS IN YOUR NOTES, USE THE PROPER TERMS.

CROWN
CREST
EYE
CHEEK
BEAK OR BILL
NECK
THROAT
BACK
BREAST
WING
FLANK
RUMP
BELLY
TAIL
FOOT
LEG

FIELD MARKS

Streaks, spots, or large patches of color are called field marks. Some field marks, such as eye and neck rings or breast streaks, are visible all the time. Wing and tail field marks may show only when a bird's wing or tail feathers are spread.

During a field trip, use a notebook to quickly jot down the names of birds you see and can identify. After a field trip, try to remember how many different birds you identified by shape alone and how many you recognized by their distinctive field marks.

Knowing the typical parts of a bird and spotting field marks will make it easier for you to describe what you've seen to other people.

BOTH MALE AND FEMALE HOODED MERGANSERS
HAVE CRESTS. AN ADDITIONAL FIELD MARK
IS THE MALE'S BRIGHT WHITE "HOOD."

♀

♂

ANY BRIGHT PATCHES
MAKE GOOD
FIELD MARKS.

MYRTLE
WARBLERS
HAVE
YELLOW
RUMPS.

CAPE PETREL

THE SOLITARY
VIREO'S WHITE
EYE RINGS ARE
MORE SUBTLE
FIELD MARKS.

SOMETIMES A BIRD'S MOST DISTINCTIVE
FIELD MARK IS NOT A MARK AT ALL, BUT
THE WAY IT HOLDS OR MOVES ITS TAIL.

RUDDY DUCKS OFTEN
HOLD THEIR TAIL
FEATHERS UPRIGHT.

PHOEBES HABITUALLY
PUMP THEIR TAILS.

♂ = MALE   ♀ = FEMALE

RED-BREASTED NUTHATCH PREPARING TO CRACK OPEN A SEED ON A BRANCH.

CROW ON LOOKOUT

BIRD BEHAVIOR

Bird-watching is more than identifying the birds you see. It is also watching the things birds do—how they find food, how they use their bills or beaks to eat, and how they react to their natural enemies. A bird-watching field trip could focus specifically on finding out where birds build their nests or how they find nest materials. A bird-watcher can spend whole days out-doors learning how different birds raise their young and how they protect their babies from danger.

PINE SISKINS SHARING A FEEDER.

Birds have many enemies. They must be vigilant. They aggressively protect their young. For your safety and the security of the birds, always stay at least twenty feet away from nesting birds. Use your binoculars to see them up close. Never climb up in a tree or on a ladder to see into a bird nest built high off the ground. Bird parents will swoop and dive at you to drive you away and may cause you to fall. If you are on the ground looking up at a bird nest and one or both of the parent birds begins diving at you, back away; you are obviously too close.

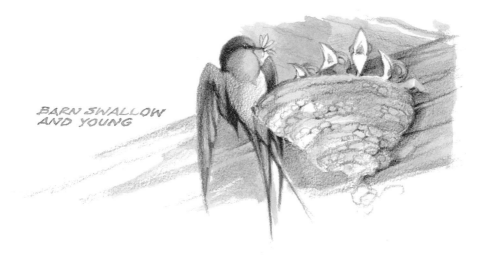

BARN SWALLOW AND YOUNG

KEEPING A NOTEBOOK

The notes I make in the field determine further reading I may want to do at home or in the library, or what I might look for regarding birds on the Internet. Field-trip notes can be a treasure chest of wonders and questions you and your fellow field trippers can research together.

On your field trip, use at least one full page in your notebook for each bird sighting. First, record the day and time. Next, record the place you saw the bird. Was it in a field or near the water? Was it on a grassy lawn or in a woodlot? You might want to add a brief sentence describing the feature by which you identified the bird—its color, shape, or field mark. Do a small sketch of the bird and make notes about the bird's behavior. You can squeeze a lot of information on one page.

AUGUST 8   7:00 AM   AT THE POND

THIS MORNING I SAW A GREAT BLUE
HERON IN THE CATTAIL CORNER
OF THE POND.

AT FIRST IT HAD IT'S
NECK ALL SCRUNCHED
DOWN AND I COULDN'T
TELL WHAT BIRD IT WAS.

THEN IT
STRETCHED TALL
AND I COULD TELL
IT WAS A HERON.

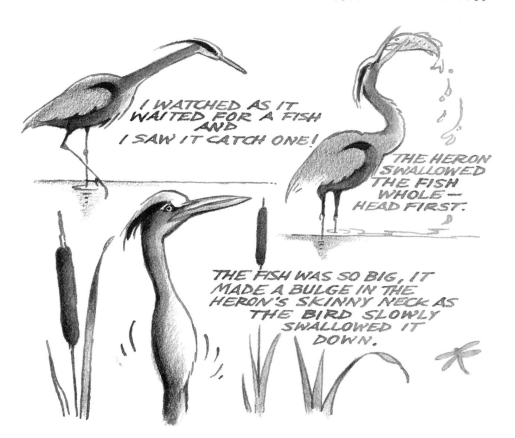

I WATCHED AS IT
WAITED FOR A FISH
AND
I SAW IT CATCH ONE!

THE HERON
SWALLOWED
THE FISH
WHOLE —
HEAD FIRST.

THE FISH WAS SO BIG, IT
MADE A BULGE IN THE
HERON'S SKINNY NECK AS
THE BIRD SLOWLY
SWALLOWED IT
DOWN.

63

You can make notebook entries that record specific observations and information about birds.

WHENEVER A BIRD SPREADS ITS WINGS
AND LOWERS THEM TO THE GROUND,
IT IS A SIGN OF AGGRESSION,

WHETHER TO DEFEND TERRITORY

OR TO HOARD FOOD.

THIS AGGRESSIVE ACTION IS KNOWN
AS MANTLING.

IN MANY SPECIES OF BIRDS, MALES (♂) AND FEMALES (♀) LOOK ALIKE.

IN SPECIES WHERE MALES AND FEMALES DIFFER, EVEN SLIGHTLY, THE MORE COLORFUL OF THE PAIR IS THE MALE...

...EXCEPT IN THE CASE OF THE BELTED KINGFISHER. THE FEMALE BELTED KINGFISHER IS MORE COLORFUL THAN THE MALE.

FEMALE HAS AN ORANGE BELT.

RARE BIRD SIGHTINGS

Contact your local Audubon Society and find out which birds in your area are considered to be rare or endangered species. You, your family, or your class at school can choose a bird as a special project and always keep an eye out for it. Remember to let the Audubon Society know if you see one!

MY OWN PARTICULAR FAVORITE IS THE OSPREY.

HERE ARE THREE OTHER RARE SPECIES TO LOOK FOR:

PEREGRINE FALCON

BALD EAGLE

IVORY-BILLED WOODPECKER.
[OUR RAREST BIRD!]
NOTE DOUBLE WHITE WING BARS

Was that a hawk or a crow?

Even while riding in the car or school bus, there are birds to be seen. The most commonly seen roadside birds are hawks and crows. Since hawks and crows are nearly the same size, it is sometimes hard to tell which is which. Here is one instance where it is easy to distinguish a hawk from a crow, even at a distance.

A HAWK, LIKE ALL OTHER BIRDS OF PREY, CARRIES FOOD CLUTCHED IN IT'S SHARP TALONS.

A CROW ALWAYS CARRIES FOOD IN ITS BILL.

SEE HOW MANY OTHER DIFFERENCES YOU CAN FIND BY OBSERVING THESE TWO COMMON ROADSIDE BIRDS.

DUCKS FLY IN SMALL GROUPS
WITH NO APPARENT LEADER

SMALL BIRDS FLOCK IN A CROWD

JAY

CROW

Of course, the easiest way to identify distant birds is by their distinctive shapes. Here are the birds most often identified by shape alone. Memorize a few before each field trip. Before long, you'll know them all at a glance. Happy bird-watching!

CORMORANT

GULL

TERN

PLOVER

SANDPIPER

IBIS

PELICAN

"GEESE FLY IN "V" FORMATION

EAGLE

VULTURE

HAWK

FALCON

KESTREL

CRANE

HERON

EGRET

69

KINGFISHER

BLUEBIRD

CHICKADEE

CARDINAL

NUTHATCH

WOODPECKER

THRASHER

ROBIN [THRUSH]

OWLS

TURKEY

QUAIL

PHEASANT

ROADRUNNER

70

PIGEON

BARN SWALLOW

DOVE

CAVE SWALLOW

HUMMINGBIRD

TREE SWALLOW

WREN

LOON

GREBE

GOOSE

DUCK

SWAN

WOOD DUCK

72

4

SHORE WALKING

I have spent many hours at the water's edge admiring, wondering, reaching in, and getting wet. I love the way a brook meanders down a wooded hillside. I like following the irregular shoreline of a natural pond or lake.

Many significant firsts in my outdoor life have occurred on some shoreline. While playing on the sandy bank of a narrow brook, I saw my first wild deer. On the rocky edge of a mountain stream, I saw my first wild trout. From a shoreline blind made of sticks and leaves, I photographed my first wood duck. And while exploring around a beaver pond, I observed my first black bear, out standing in the shallow water where it was feeding on tall grasses.

Shore walkers are always making new discoveries. Animal tracks on the wet shore are invariably fresh. Interesting objects such as driftwood, colorful stones, and shells are constantly washing in. Some of the best field trips skirt or follow a shoreline.

If, like me, you are irresistibly drawn to water, love the feel of sand or smooth stones under your feet, and enjoy nothing better than watching sunlight play on the surface of a wave . . . you are a shore walker through and through.

TROUT AND MAYFLY

Wherever water—salt or fresh—meets land, things get interesting. Shoreland is the end of the world for terrestrial creatures and the beginning of the mysterious underworld of aquatic life.

SANDPIPER

TYPES OF SHORELAND

Shoreland can be as rugged and unapproachable as a rocky coast or as smooth and accessible as a sandy beach. It can be clearly defined, such as pond water lapping against mud banks. Or it can be a series of subtle changes, like those from open water to marsh to dry land. A shore walker has a variety of places to explore.

THE ROCKY NEW ENGLAND SEA-COAST IS FAMOUS FOR ITS RUGGED CHARACTER, BUT...

CAUTION: ROCKY SHORES SUCH AS THIS ARE BEST OBSERVED WITH BINOCULARS FROM A SAFE DISTANCE ON FIRM, WELL-TRAVELED PATHS.

PLANT SUCCESSION

On shores that gradually change first to marsh, then to drier land, you will notice a pattern of plant succession.

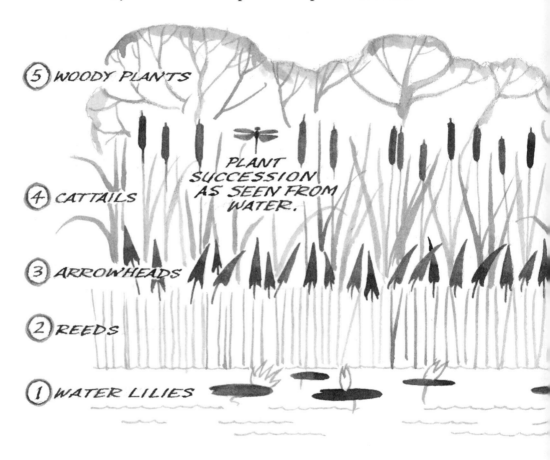

⑤ WOODY PLANTS

PLANT SUCCESSION AS SEEN FROM WATER.

④ CATTAILS

③ ARROWHEADS

② REEDS

① WATER LILIES

Low aquatic plants give way to taller ones—lilies to reeds to arrowheads to cattails; and beyond the cattails, water-loving willows or alders.

The best way to see this is not from shore but from the water, either in a canoe or while wading slowly in firm-bottomed shallows.

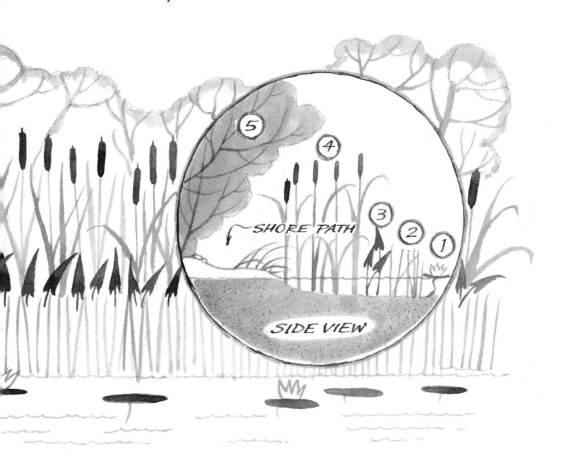

SHORE PATH

SIDE VIEW

Once you recognize basic shoreline plant successions, you will be better able to record your shore sightings in your notes.

Water attracts wildlife. Even the most shy forest creatures come to shorelines to drink or hunt for food in the shallow water. Shore walkers see the greatest variety of birds—perching birds, such as warblers and sparrows; shore walking or wading birds, including turnstones, herons, egrets and yellowlegs, and swimming ducks and grebes.

PIED~BILLED
GREBE

GREATER
YELLOWLEGS

RUDDY TURNSTONE

YELLOWTHROAT
WARBLER

A RACCOON FEELING
AROUND FOR CRAYFISH

Look for deer and raccoon tracks in the shoreline mud. Watch for frogs, salamanders, water snakes, and turtles living on shore. In shallow water, fish can be observed stalking and catching aquatic insects.

BULLFROG

DAMSELFLY

SPOTTED
SALAMANDER

SHORE-WALKING SAFETY

There are some places where shore walking is simply not advisable. In areas where alligators and/or venomous snakes live, the water's edge is a place where the reptiles sun themselves or hide to strike at water-loving prey. In parts of the country where such danger lurks in and around water, I confine my walking to boardwalks or the higher ground of established trails.

CLEARLY PRESSED DEER TRACKS USUALLY INDICATE FIRM GROUND. HOWEVER, CLEAR FOOTPRINTS OF SMALL ANIMALS AND BIRDS DO NOT NECESSARILY MEAN THE GROUND IS SAFE FOR YOU TO WALK ON.

As always in the Great Outdoors, be careful where you go. Thoroughly test soft shoreland with a strong stick to make sure you won't sink in when walking. Use the stick to retest the softness of ground as you go.

I only wade in very shallow water, and only where the bottom is firm. At the seashore, unless I'm with a guide who is familiar with the changing tide, I never wander out to exposed reefs or sandbars—places that a high tide can flood rather quickly.

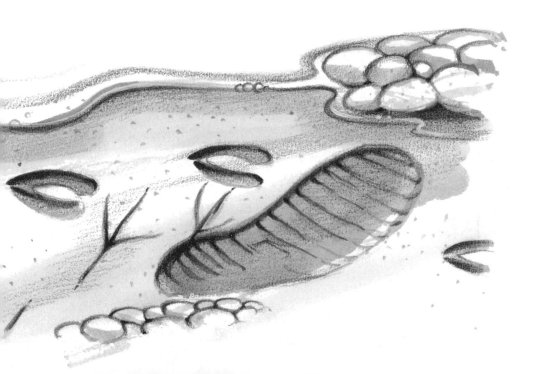

A SHORE WALKER'S NOTEBOOK

Keeping a record of shore walks will help you remember the best places to walk, where you saw a snake sunning, etc. A shore walker's notebook can also be a record of unexpected happenings. Once, while sketching in my notebook on the coast of Maine, a surprisingly energetic wave sent a spray of water over me and my notebook. Salt water blurred and smeared much of what I had written and drawn. Even so, it has become one of my favorite notebook entries.

By making small sketches of everything you find interesting—stones, plants, shed insect skins—you'll capture the details of a place forever. If you see any wildlife, sketch it quickly and then circle it or draw a box around it to make it special. To show proper proportions in a tiny sketch of a scene, add a self portrait. I do it all the time in my notebook. It's fun!

SAMPLE NOTEBOOK PAGE

OCT. 23   CRINKLE COVE
                          WATER CALM, AIR WARM.

LATE THIS EVENING, WHILE WALKING
ALONG THE SHORE, I SPOTTED AN
UNUSUAL FISH FOR OUR COVE.
IT WAS A WARMOUTH.

THE FISH WAS
VERY CLOSE TO SHORE

WARMOUTH

HERE ARE SOME OTHER THINGS I SAW.

KILLIFISH
[4"]

WATER BOATMAN
[ON WATER SURFACE]

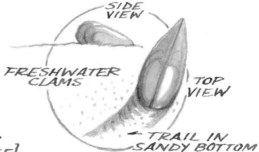

SIDE
VIEW

FRESHWATER
CLAMS

TOP
VIEW

← TRAIL IN
SANDY BOTTOM

ALL THIS IN WATER ONLY INCHES DEEP!

FOUND OBJECTS

Shore walkers are always finding some interesting object they simply must bring home as a memento of the day. Tiny pieces of driftwood are beautiful to look at and, when allowed to dry, make great shelf decorations. Rocks with veins of quartz running through are shoreline gems. Bring home rocks of different types of stone such as sandstone, shale, and granite. At the seashore, seashells are the objects most sought after, and finding a new kind is always exciting. Remember, shells are the outer coverings of living creatures. Any shell you find that looks still occupied should be returned to the sea.

The best shores for shell seekers are those that are in the path of hurricanes. Hurricanes churn up the sea bottom so thoroughly, offshore shells that have settled and become buried are uncovered and pushed to shore. As soon as a hurricane blows by and it is once again safe to go on the beach, the shell collectors are out, combing the wind-blown sand for special treasures.

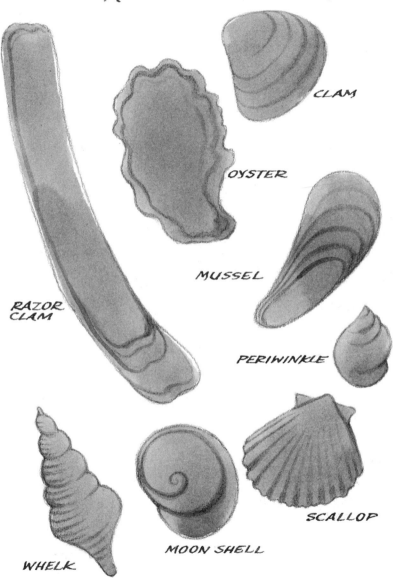

COMMON SEASHELLS
[IDENTIFICATION SILHOUETTES]

CLAM

OYSTER

MUSSEL

RAZOR
CLAM

PERIWINKLE

WHELK

MOON SHELL

SCALLOP

FOSSIL FINDS

Many inland waters were once part of a saltwater sea. Evidence of this can be found in random shoreline stones containing fascinating fossil forms of long-gone sea creatures.

SEASHELL FOSSILS

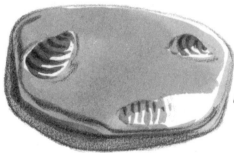

TRILOBITES
[EXTINCT MARINE ARTHROPODS]

ENTIRE FISH FOSSIL – A RARE FIND!

UNDERWATER PLANTS

On shores where you can see down into water at least one foot deep, look for these common freshwater submerged plants. On windy days, look for the same plants washed ashore, torn free from their underwater roots by rough waves.

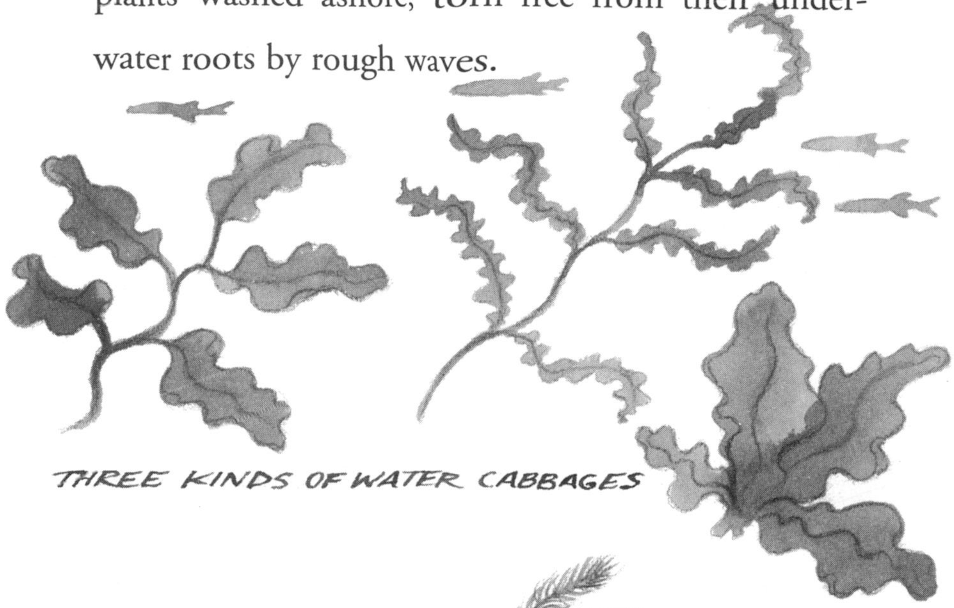

THREE KINDS OF WATER CABBAGES

WATER MILFOIL

COONTAIL

EELGRASS

SHORELINE TREES

Of course, every shore walker should look up from the shoreline once in a while to appreciate the great variety of trees that grow along the water. This last group of silhouette charts will help you identify most of the trees and shoreline plants you see.

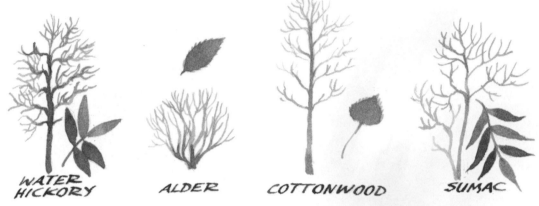

WATER HICKORY   ALDER   COTTONWOOD   SUMAC

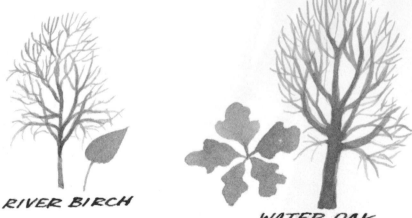

RIVER BIRCH   WATER OAK

NOTE: TREES SHOWN IN SIZE PROPORTION TO ONE ANOTHER.

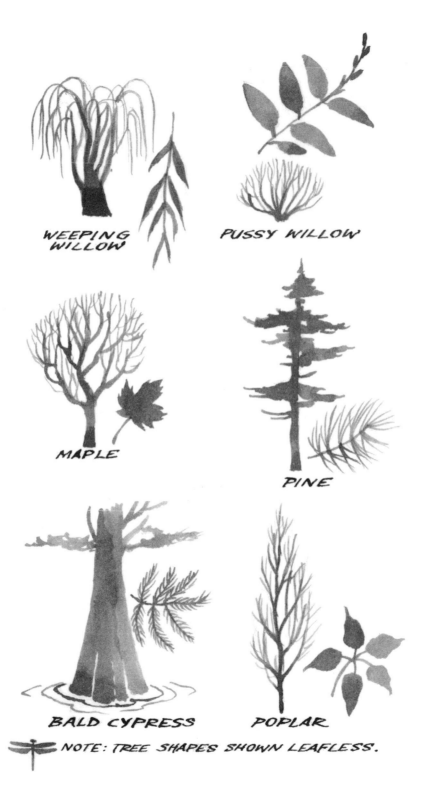

WEEPING
WILLOW

PUSSY WILLOW

MAPLE

PINE

BALD CYPRESS

POPLAR

NOTE: TREE SHAPES SHOWN LEAFLESS.

91

In my work as a wildlife artist, I get to go on a field trip every day! But my favorite field trips are those I share with my nature-loving family. Share this book with your family, friends, and classmates. Use it to plan your outings and take it along. It can help you get where you want to go, see what you hope to see, and learn the many things in nature you wish to know.

INDEX

alligators, 40–41, 82
animal tracks, 30–51
  of cats and dogs, 39, 49
  dew claws in, 46
  freshness of, 44–45
  in hopping, walking,
    running, 36–37
  notebook for, 42–43
  safety in looking for,
    40–41
  sets of, 34–35
  unique types of, 38
ants, 15, 26
aquatic bugs, 13, 28–29,
  81, 85
arachnids, 10, 13, 29
armadillo, 48
arrowheads (plants),
  78–79, 93

badger, 49
bears, 37, 41, 45, 49, 73
beaver, 35, 48
bees, 15, 18–19, 26
beetles, 27, 29
binoculars, 15, 61, 76
birds, 52–71, 80
  behavior of, 60–61, 67
  field marks of, 58–59
  male and female, 65
  mantling by, 64
  nests of, 61
  notebook for, 58, 62–65
  rare, sightings of, 66

  terms for parts of,
    56–57
  tracks of, 33, 34, 50–51
bluebird, 70
blue jay, 34, 50, 68
bobcat, 39, 49
bugs, 8–29
  cases, cocoons, and
    chrysalises of, 22–23
  definition of, 10
  equipment for hunting,
    14–15
  night hunting of, 24–25
  notebook for, 20–21
  number of legs of, 10
  three main groups of,
    13
bullrushes, 93
butterflies, 11, 23, 25

caddis flies, 22–23, 26, 28
cardinal, 56, 70
caterpillars, 11, 23, 27
cats, 34, 39, 49
cattails, 78–79, 93
chickadee, 70
chipmunk, 50
chrysalises, 22–23
cicadas, 27
clams, 85, 87
clothes for tall grass or
  weeds, 16
cockroaches, 27
cocoons, 22–23

cormorant, 68
cougar, 35, 41, 49
cow, 48
coyote, 49
cranes, 51, 69
crickets, 27
crows, 50, 60, 67, 68

deer, 32, 38, 42–43, 45,
  48, 73, 82–83
dew claws, 46
dogs, 39, 45, 49
doves, 71
dragonfly, 8, 18, 20–21,
  26, 28
ducks, 51, 57, 59, 68,
  71–73

eagles, 66, 69
earwig, 27
egret, 69
elk, 48

falcons, 66, 69
fish, 85, 88
flies, 26, 74, 81
fossil finds, 88
foxes, 32, 38–39, 49
frogs, 81

geese, 51, 69, 71
gnat, 28
grasshoppers, 19, 27
grebes, 71, 80

grouse, 32, 33, 51
grubs, 27
gulls, 51, 68

hawks, 67, 69
herons, 51, 63, 69
hornets, 15, 26
horse, 48
houseplants, 12
hummingbirds, 71
hurricanes, 86

ibis, 68
insect repellant, 16

kestrel, 69
kingfisher, 65, 70

ladybug, 12
larvae, 22–23, 28
lizards, 47
loon, 71
lynx, 49

mantids, 27
mealybug, 27
mergansers, 59
mink, 49
mite, 29
monarch butterfly, 11, 23
moose, 41, 45, 46, 48
mosquitoes, 28
moths, 23, 25
mouse, 35, 50
muskrat, 35, 48

nuthatches, 60, 70

osprey, 66

otter, 35, 49
owls, 51, 70

peccary, 48
pelican, 68
petrels, 59
pheasant, 70
phoebes, 59
pigeon, 51, 71
pine siskins, 60
plants
    growing through water
        surface, 93
    shoreland, 92
    shoreline, 78–79
    underwater, 89
plover, 68
porcupine, 48
possum, 48

quail, 70

rabbits, 32, 36, 45, 50
raccoon, 32, 38, 48, 81
reptiles, 82
    tracks of, 40–41, 47
roadrunner, 51, 70
robin, 70
ruddy turnstone, 80

salamanders, 81
sandpiper, 68, 75
scorpion, 29
seashells, 86–87
sheep, 48
shoreland, types of, 76–77
shore walking, 72–93
    notebook for, 84–85
    safety in, 82–83

skunk, 38, 49
snakes, 47, 81, 82
snow, tracking in, 33,
    44–45
sparrow, 50, 55
spiders, 12, 29
squirrels, 50
swallows, 61, 71
swans, 51, 71

tail drags, 35, 47, 50
termites, 28
terns, 68
thrasher, 70
ticks, 16–17, 29
trees, shoreline, 90–91
trilobites, 88
trout, 73, 74
turkey, 51, 70
turtles, 47, 81

vireos, 59
vole, 50
vultures, 69

walking stick, 27
warblers, 59, 80
wasps, 18–19, 26
water lilies, 78–79, 93
weasel, 49
weevils, 27
wolf, 45, 49
wolverine, 49
woodcock, 51
woodpeckers, 52, 55, 66,
    70
wrens, 71

yellowlegs, 80